W9-AEF-389

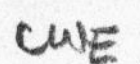


# Writing 16

CHARLES OLSON

# Causal Mythology

Four Seasons Foundation

San Francisco: 1969

Grateful acknowledgment is made to Corinth Books for permission to reprint several of *The Maximus Poems* read in the course of the lecture, to the Bollingen Foundation for permission to reprint a paragraph from Henry Corbin's *Avicenna and the Visionary Recital* (translated from the French by Willard R. Trask, Copyright 1960 by Bollingen Foundation), and to Hans Güterbock and *Journal of Cuneiform Studies* for permission to reprint part of his translation of "The Song of Ullikummi."

Library of Congress Catalog Card Number: 67-19579

Cover photograph by Steamboat

The Writing Series is edited by Donald Allen, and published by Four Seasons Foundation
Distributed by City Lights Books, 1562 Grant Avenue, San Francisco, California 94133

# Causal Mythology

A lecture delivered to the University of California Poetry Conference, July 20, 1965, at Berkeley.

The editor wishes to thank Brian Fawcett and Albert Glover for letting him compare their transcriptions with his own; and acknowledges his indebtedness to Robin Blaser, George Butterick, Brian Fawcett, and David Schaff for their help in identifying sources cited in the notes.

ROBERT DUNCAN:

Some things in poetry are matters of appreciation; literary values or social values or aesthetic values that do not vitally concern me. And some things are matters of taste, of my liking or not liking them in part or in total. These have no solid ground in the truth of things for me. But I had occasion only recently to give testimony to something that was a matter of fact for me. In a passage in his preface to *Prometheus Unbound*, Shelley tells us "one great poet is a masterpiece of nature which another not only ought to study but must study." As to the work of what poets stand in this order for me, I have no doubts. This is no longer a matter of what I may or may not, ought to or ought not to, feel, but what I have had to study.

There were—now that Williams is dead, and H.D. dead, there *are* five poets left that I study. I know I must study them because at every turn I am back at those texts in order to get at the information I need, to find something that is not a matter of literature but of my own inner reality of life. These five were very clearly, three I feel are superiors, for I find in their mastery of the craft and their depth of thought and feeling challenge beyond my own craft and depths: Ezra Pound, Louis Zukofsky, Charles Olson; and then two I feel are peers and companions, for in their craft and their depth they have increased my share: Robert Creeley and Denise Levertov.

I return to find secrets, I return to *rob* them, you know. If I had to steal fire I know where to go, and there isn't any doubt. Everywhere else I might be stealing anything. I am a jackdaw in poetry. But I know when I'm coming home with a piece of colored glass that I've found that fits the design, and where to go for the fire at the center of things. For all of the poets who matter to me in my generation Charles Olson has been a Big Fire Source. One of the ones we have had to study.

CHARLES OLSON:

You know I'm very obliged to get rid of that rap for being Zeus. I never knew I was Prometheus until now. It's a fine thing—I've been a father figure too long. [Laughter.] And I've begun to suffer so completely the fate of that other fellow that what I propose to do today is to expose myself, as he was, on a rock. And, in fact, if I can accomplish anything it's simply because there's a little of my liver left from overnight, like I think his was. [Laughter.]

In fact, what I would like to do, actually, is to do that sort of a thing, I mean, the announced subject was Causal Mythology, so obviously Mr. Duncan has prepared me perfectly. And it's very exciting to be home here, at least it feels strange and nice to be in Berkeley this morning. Especially because so many of you here are the ones that I've lived mostly for, and with, and by, myself, and care the most for in the world.

It's very strange because I suddenly was presented to Ezra Pound two weeks ago, after twenty years. And that was like—I don't know—it was not like your father or something—it was like having an Umbrian angel suddenly descend upon you and ask you to be and be more than, well, just what you'd like to be. It was very beautiful the way the fierceness of Pound has settled down into a voiceless thing which only responded twice to me. Once I told a story of Ed Sanders, who had a beautiful picture that Pound at eighty would have a revival of life and have fifteen further years of power. The difficulty of talking to Pound is he doesn't talk anymore. He sits in an almost catatonic fix in silence. And the one word he said after I said that Sanders had that sense of him, he said, "Sanders has a sense of humor." [Laughter.]

The thing that I *would* like to do instead of what sounds like a subject, like Causal Mythology, is actually to talk four things:

The Earth
The Image of the World
The History or City
and The Spirit of the World

and do those four things under an epigraph which would be:

*that which exists through itself is what is called meaning.*

And the reason why I say that is the desire to suggest that the four terms that I am proposing are—the Earth itself, for example, is curiously today a thing which can be seen for itself. And I think that that's so completely changed the human species, literally, that it's almost like the old blessing of the pope, that it is an *orb*—and, in fact, I likewise am pairing the city, which if you remember in his blessing was the *urb,* as that pair. And the other pair I'd like to call instead, in Latin, the *imago mundi* and the *anima mundi.* And in doing this I would like to use four poems: —there are four poems written, in fact, in a run, and I'll read them not that way but read them in a series, and see if by casting the relationship of, say, the four terms to the four poems will not destroy the poems. These will all be from the *Maximus,* written about a year ago. Some have been published. The first one is an attempt, actually a further attempt to speak my own sense at that date of the condition of the earth.

Astride
the Cabot
fault,

one leg upon the Ocean one leg
upon the Westward drifting continent,

to build out of sound the wall
of a city,

the earth
rushing westward 2′
each 100
years, 300 years past
500 years
since Cabot, stretching
the Ocean, the earth

going NNW, course due
W from north of the
Azores, St. Martin's
Land,

the division
increasing yet the waters
of the Atlantic
lap the shore, the history

of the nation rushing to melt
in the Mongolian ice, to arrive
at Frances Rose-Troup Land, novoye

Sibersky
slovo,

the Wall
to arise from the River, the Diorite Stone
to be lopped off the Left Shoulder[1]

Now deliberately I'd like to go over it, almost like an exegesis of text, if you'll excuse me. As I said, I have arrived at a point where I really have no more than to feed on myself. Unfortunately I didn't bring a *Maximus Poems*. Would anybody have one? That I could borrow? Thanks. I'd like very much to literally do a—for example that "Francis Rose-Troup Land,"[2] and that "Mongolian ice" stuff. I'd love to just talk about the Earth in these terms. I did do an earlier passage on this particular English woman historian in a poem called "Letter, May 2, 1959"—I'll pick a section out of it: "then to now nothing/ new"—that would be from the seventeenth-century persons referred to just previously.

then to now nothing
new, in the meaning
that that wall walked
today, happened a bull-
dozer discloses
Meeting House Hill
was a sanddune under
what was valued for
still the sun makes
a west here as on
each Gloucester hill

why one can say what
one can't say is

when did the sea so
roll over as later
the ice this stuck-out
10 miles Europe-pointing
cape, the lines of force
I said to her as of Rose-
Troup go to as one line
as taught as uroboros ar-
row hooped crazy Zen arch-
er fact that arm of bow Frances
Rose-Troup English maiden
lady told this city what[3]

And then it goes on into *what* she told Gloucester about how persons first got there. Now this thing goes on to—well, let me read that, because that is my point of the relevance of taking the Earth as a *One*—by the old law that a one is only so if it produces a one. This would be, then, if you talk a Causal Mythology, the simplicity of the principle "that which exists through itself is what is called meaning"—will be that one produces a one. The Earth, then, is conceivably a knowable, a seizable, a single, and *your* thing. And yours as a single thing and person yourself, not something that's distributed simply because we are so many and the population is growing, or that the exploitation of the earth itself is increasing. The:

. . . fact that arm of bow Frances
Rose-Troup English maiden
lady told this city what

marchants Weymouth Port Book
No. 873 if East and West the
ship first employed was,
the date everything that
the local get off it Glous-
ter the old railroad joke
from the smell, the lovers

in the back seat the conductor
waking up from a snooze don't
look out the window sniffs
and calls out gloucester glous-
ter    All off

Take the top off
Meeting House Hill
is 128 has cut it
on two sides

the third
is now no more than
more Riverdale
Park

and the fourth?
the west?
is the rubbish
of white man

Up River,
under the bridge
the summer people
kid themselves
there's no noise,
the Bridge
's so high.
Like hell. The Diesels
shake the sky

clean the earth
of sentimental
drifty dirty
lazy man:

bulldozer,
lay open
the sand some sea

was all over the
second third fourth
meeting house,

once. I take my air

where Eveleth walked
out the west
on these hills
because the river

it's earth which
now is strange The sea
is east The choice Our backs
turned from the sea but the smell

as the minister said
in our noses
I am interfused
with the rubbish

of creation I hear
the necessity
of the ludicrous reference to Wm Hubbard by the
tercentennary preacher that

the finny tribe come easily
to the hook

Fishermen
are killers Every
fifty of 'em I pick off
the Records seek
the kame I was raised
on and are startled,
as I am, by each granite
morraine shape    Am in the mud
off Five Pound Island
is the grease-pit
of State Pier

Go 'way and leave
Rose-Troup and myself   I smell your breath, sea
And unmellowed River under
the roar of A. Piatt Andrew
hung up there like fission
dropping trucks the face
Samuel Hodgkins didn't show
poling pulling 1 penny
per person 2
for a horse

step off
onto the nation   The sea
will rush over   The ice
will drag boulders   Commerce
was changed the fathometer
was invented here the present
is worse give nothing now your credence
start all over step off the
Orontes onto land no Typhon
no understanding of a cave
a mystery Cashes? . . . . "but that these times of combustion
the seas throughout have hindered much that work" so sayeth
so early[4]

And then it jibes, and I want to still come to that passage where I get this same siberskie slovo job . . . Wait a minute . . . [Looks through the text.] No. I can't. Well, I don't know how I lost that one. It sure was there once. Well, it's somewhere.[5]

I want to go back now, really building, coming back to that original poem that I read. In fact, I'm really trying to explain that I don't believe I'm obscure. [Laughter.] In fact, really, I enjoy these terms so much that I obviously, as I said, have no reason not to try to explain them or, this day at least, lay them open to you. Let me go over the poem again and at least allow—oh yes, really, I *can* do it by catching the passage where, earlier in that poem:

Mellow and enclosed both the local and the past
N.G. not the point not here I am not here to

have to do with Englishmen (in habit, but
canoes dugout as found Indian means or hauling
marsh grass by gundalows possibly old Venetian

who came out of their marshes likewise
to change the commerce of NW shifting
man—it ends, as Stefansson couldn't
stomach the dead end of his own prop-
osition, in the ice

dogs of the present don't even throw anything back The sea
it isn't 67 years yet that the First Parish (Unitarian) preacher of the anniversary sermon . . .[6]

And so forth. So I'm really suggesting how much this poem, which was written in 59, is very loaded, again, simply because, say, I find myself constantly returning to that unit, Earth as orb, as though it was as familiar to me as the smallest thing I know, and it's really, actually, to suggest that if there is any legitimacy to the word that we call mythology it is literally the activeness, the possible activeness and personalness of experiencing it as such.

Astride
the Cabot
fault,

one leg upon the Ocean one leg
upon the Westward drifting continent,

to build out of sound the wall
of a city,

the earth
rushing westward 2'
each 100
years, 300 years past
500 years
since Cabot, stretching
the Ocean, the earth

going NNW, course due
W from north of the
Azores, St. Martin's
Land,

the division
increasing yet the waters
of the Atlantic
lap the shore, the history

of the nation rushing to melt
in the Mongolian ice, to arrive
at Frances Rose-Troup Land, novoye

Sibersky
slovo,

the Wall
to arise from the River, the Diorite Stone
to be lopped off the Left Shoulder[7]

By the way, I'd be happy to be interrupted on any of each one of these four parts this thing will constitute itself as. At the moment I'm running part one out. But I'd be happy to be picked over by anybody that wants, who is unfamiliar or is unsatisfied with any of either the information or this other thing that I'm trying to do which is the connectivity of same to other poems of the *Maximus* at least.

BOBBIE CREELEY:

What do you mean by "the Diorite Stone lopped off the Left Shoulder"?

CHARLES OLSON:

Yeah. That I would like, Bobbie, to hold a little back because of the fourth of the: I do have a board, don't I. [Olson writes the following on the blackboard:

| | | |
|---|---|---|
| (1) THE EARTH— | ORB | TRADE, UGLY, RATIONAL |
| (2) IMAGO MUNDI | | ENYALION, BEAUTY IS WAR |
| (3) HISTORY— | URB | POLITICS, POLIS—JOHN WANAX |
| (4) ANIMA MUNDI | | IKUNTA LULI—WOMAN |

Some words on the right were added later during the course of the lecture.] Can everybody see that?

The first poem that I read is called "Astride the Cabot Fault." I learned that, by the way, luckily in Vancouver, from one of the Vancouver people that I think isn't here today, Dan McLeod. He showed me in Vancouver a thing which I had never realized, that there's a split in the Atlantic Ocean, a fault which runs just where all my own attention has been—northeast—and that she runs right straight through Gloucester. This was, for him, very exciting. [Laughter.] It's again, like, by the principle of the *imago mundi* or the Prometheus figure, you get stuck with all this stuff. I wouldn't propose what I'm proposing to anybody because you end up obviously being eaten by Zeus' eagle only, and you're nobody, you're not even a hero. You're simply stuck with the original visionary experience of having been *you,* which is a hell of a thing. [Laughter.] And, in fact, I assume that the epigraph that I've offered today is my only way of supporting that, which is [he writes on the board]: *that which exists through itself is what is called meaning.* All right?

I don't have any trouble stealing that, as Duncan never has any trouble stealing because he has a visional experience which prompts him to reach out for just what he knows he wants. I was very lucky once to have what poets call visions. And they're not dreams, as several superb poets in this room know. They are literally either given things or voices which come to you from cause. I won't quote, as one never does, one's own secrets, that's why you steal from others. But this one is an awfully good duplication. And the reason, Bobbie, I'd like very much to wait on—no, I can answer the question very well.

The Diorite, uh . . . in fact, wow, this is marvelous, Allen [Ginsberg]. I'll read the one that you, for the first time, came on in Vancouver. That's a fun, huh? It was that one? Yeah. If you remember, Bobbie, I did read a poem in Vancouver which has me as the Diorite Stone on Main Street. And now if I could just hit it and read it, but if I could I would . . . [Looks through MS.] I can't remember the damn thing! I don't know where it is. Hold on. The advantage, by the way, of coming in fresh is that even if you're unprepared it's more fun for me. I hope you won't mind my dragging a little. "I stand on Main Street like the Diorite Stone," as I remember it.

I'm going to spend some time in this fourth thing on the poem from which I myself steal that, which is "The Song of Ullikummi." Actually it comes to us as a Hittite version of a Hurrian myth. It's called "The Song of Ullikummi." And it's the story of how this aborted creature, whom the poem calls the Diorite Stone, started growing from the bottom of the sea, and grew until he appeared above the surface of the water and then, of course, attention was called to him and he continued to grow and he became so offensive to the gods, and dangerous, that they had to, themselves, do battle with him. "The Song of Ullikummi" is actually the story of that battle and who could bring him down. Because he had a growth principle of his own, and it went against creation in the sense that nobody could stop him and nobody knew how far he might grow. It's a marvelous Hesiodic poem. In fact, I prefer it to those passages in Hesiod that include the battle of Zeus with the giants and eventually with Typhon, because this creature is nothing but a blue stone, and the *stone* grows. I would hate to start talking mythology except to mention that American Indians, the Sioux, for example, believe that a stone is—I mean that Crazy Bear or someone of them, whichever was the old guy that said it, but he does say that the stone is the truest condition of creation, that it is silence and it is solidity and all that. Well, I like that. I mean, I think the Earth is nothing but a pebble, a marvelously big stone. Big Stone. Why not? Let's call the Earth "Big Stone." And the Diorite, for me, this Diorite figure is the vertical, the growth principle of the Earth. He's just an objectionable child of Earth who has got no condition except earth, no condition but stone. And, as you know, in alchemy this is great stuff, the lapis and all that, but one of the reasons why I'm trying to even beat the old dead word "mythology" into meaning is that I think that it holds more of a poet's experience than any meaning the word "mysticism" holds. The principle would seem to be that the only interest of a spiritual exercise is production.

QUESTION:

What's the "lopped off the Left Shoulder"?

CHARLES OLSON:

Yeah. Well this is how he finally was destroyed. I've forgotten which one of the younger gods, but it would be a character again like Prometheus, who finally took on—the old boys couldn't handle it, the women were all upset. That was cutting out, by the way, organic principles. Biomorphism is absolutely knocked flat by this figure. I mean, we don't need any longer to put up with that business, if you could get this guy back in business. Nor do we need to put up with Zeus, either, and those big-shot figures. This young other guy, like Enki or some crazy fisherman type person, finally goes down—just like, by the way, in that beautiful early, the other poem which I still respect from prehistory is the Gilgamesh story, and here it's the opposite way. And I think we live in a time when the future lies as much in the genetic as it does in the morphological. I just happen to be a form-ridden cat myself, but I respect all that action, the other side of the whole. The right arm I respect as much as my own disabled left. I wish also today to read—well I might do that right now, as a matter of fact. Let me read you another story. I'd like to read stories today anyhow. But I'd like to read a very beautiful little story about the condition of the two angels:

> He who succeeds in leaving this clime enters the climes of the Angels, among which the one that marches with the earth is a clime in which the terrestrial angels dwell. These angels form two groups. One occupies the right side: they are the angels who know and order. Opposite them, a group occupies the left side: they are the angels who obey and act. Sometimes these two groups of angels descend to the climes of men and genii, sometimes they mount to heaven. It is said that among their number are the two angels to whom the human being is entrusted, those who are called 'Guardians and Noble Scribes'—one to the right, the other to the left. He who is to the right belongs to the angels who order; to him it falls to dictate. He who is to the left belongs to the angels who act; to him it falls to write.[8]

And, as again, I mean, I wasn't as pat as to realize I was going to read a first passage loaded on the Earth. But, again, it is why when I talk more 'intellectually' about mythology I use the word "dipolar." Well, this double that we're talking about is where this Earth thing seems to me to yield. Again the Diorite Stone is the, sort of the, child of mother Earth, dig?

I want, actually, to end by reading a poem I read, unhappily I guess, because nobody else said a word, in front of Ezra Pound two weeks ago, in honor of him. [Laughter.] It fell dead, and I'd like to read it to you today as the last poem. It's on the nature of the assault upon the rock that fathers and mothers us all, sort of thing. And it's a slipped piece of the whole story—it's from "The Song of Ullikummi." In fact, I read it as a translation, trying to honor the fact that I thought Mr. Pound really, justly, freed the languages of the world. It's interesting to me because it is a translation from Hurrian into American. Obviously that would interest me to succeed in doing that. So that "the Wall/to arise from the river, the Diorite Stone/to be lopped off the Left Shoulder" would be the, the fact—again let me go back, let's be really pedantic and do this. The wall of the city—"to build out of sound the wall/of a city," right? In the earlier second poem. "The Wall/to arise from"—the Wall here is capitalized—"the Wall/to arise from the river, the Diorite Stone/to be lopped off the Left Shoulder." In fact, as I remember—I may be clear inventing—but, as I remember the Hittite Hurrian myth, it turns out, eventually, that the damned thing that grew up was actually nothing but a carbuncle on the left shoulder—not of Atlas, but of the Earth. I mean that this thing just rose, this blue stone just rose like a skyscraper and overtopped the walls of the gods. So that they were frightened it was all going to topple down on them. As indeed I am that neo-capitalism as well as communism is going to do that to the Earth.

I steal that phrase "neo-capitalism." I don't know it as American jive. I was quite interested in a communist poet that read—in fact, I gave the stage to him in Spoleto—Pasolini, a young Italian poet. And it's very jivey talk, apparently, in Italy today, because Italy is like ourselves; it's jumped into that new gear. Don't mind my talking history and politics currently, because we have an objection to you, Allen [Ginsberg], Wieners and I. Because when we flew into Rome we said, "why don't those sons-of-bitch poets tell us how exciting experiences are?" Like just how exciting it is to fly into a city. Not that you haven't, but as a matter of fact we used you, as so many people do, as a target of *objection*. Because you don't tell us all these wonderful things, like the condition of a poet like Pasolini, talking about . . . with his *claque!* breaking up a whole damn reading in honor of Ezra Pound, rushing out and having a press conference. It was one of the worst things I've seen. Typical lousy job! [Laughter.] But the poem he read had this very exciting phrase—calling the whole present shove that's on, "neo-capitalism." It sounded marvelously true. It seems just what has happened in the last ten years. The whole world has [slaps his hands] done that big push that we call the species. But I'm old-fashioned enough to be—not scared—to *wish* that the earth shall be of another vision and another dispensation. And not from the past but from the future. OK. I didn't mean to make a pitch.

OK. I'm going to quit this Earth thing as part one, now. Jeez, I better, unless somebody wants anything more on that one poem? OK.

Now, my argument would be, then, that the way that the Earth gets to be a attained is that we are born, ourselves, with a picture of the world. That there is no world except one that we are the picturers of it. And by the world here I don't mean the Earth, I mean the whole of creation. And it seems to me that I, I don't know enough, but I think that the phrase *imago mundi* is as legitimate as the better known phrase *anima mundi.* And I'd like to oppose that, really, to a condition of writing which is based on what I do or what others do, rather than comes from the darkness of one's own initiation. Again I'm suggesting that even the overt spiritual exercise of initiation is initial in us. *We* are, *we* are, spiritual exercise, by having been born. And that this involves one in something which Blake alone, to my mind, has characterized. He, in one passage,[9] I've forgotten where, says that there's the ugly man, who would be the rational one; that there's the strong man, who would be wholly strong; that there's the beautiful man; and the fourth. And that these form the Son of God. I think I have that reasonably right.

And in the period, the day after I wrote this poem I read you first, I wrote this other poem. And it was refused by *The Paris Review,* so I'm happy to read it. [Laughter.] It's never been in print. It also is a footnote, like it's an example of another side of the literal study of mythology, which I spend a lot of time on, which is really archaeology on one side, or etymology on another. I found that in Crete, or in Greece at the time of Mycenae and Pylos and Tiryns, that the god who we know of as Ares or Mars was apparently called Enyalios. In this poem I abuse his name by using Enyalion. But the poem is based on the word Enyalion. And it's directly connected now to the struggle of the *imago mundi,* as a child of Earth, with the bosses.

I published a long poem in *The Psychedelic Review*—due to Allen [Ginsberg] I was brought into that early mushroom experience and *The Psychedelic Review* was one magazine that issued from it—and in order to, almost to put another kind of a plant in there, I put this poem. Literally, it led Ed Sanders to ask me to translate Hesiod. But I told him I knew no Greek, it was just cribbed from a good translation of Hesiod. But it does have that big war there between Zeus and the giants. And this starts from that, this is a later poem coming from there.

rages
strain
Dog of Tartarus
Guards of Tartarus
Finks of the Bosses. War Makers

not Enyalion. Enyalion
has lost his Hand, Enyalion
is beautiful, Enyalion
has shown himself, the High King
a War Chief, he has Equites
to do that

Enyalion
is possibility, all men
are the glories of Hera by possibility, Enyalion
goes to war differently
than his equites, different
than they do, he goes to war with a picture

far far out into Eternity    Enyalion,
the law of possibility, Enyalion

the beautiful one, Enyalion

who takes off his clothes

wherever he is found,

on a hill,

in front of his own troops,

in the face of the men of the other side, at the command

of any woman who goes by,

and sees him there, and sends her maid, to ask,

if he will show himself,

to see for herself,

if the beauty, of which he is reported to have,

is true

he goes to war with a picture

she goes off

in the direction of her business

over the city over the earth—the earth

is the mundus brown-red is the color

of the brilliance

of earth

he goes to war with a picture in his mind
that the shining of his body

and of the chariot
and of his horses
and of his own equites
everyone in the nation of which he is the High King

he turns back

into the battle

Enyalion

is the god of war    the color

of the god of war    is beauty

Enyalion

is in the service of the law of the proportions

of his own body    Enyalion

but the city

is only the beginning of the earth    the earth

is the world    brown-red is the color of mud,

the earth

shines

but beyond the earth

far off Stage Fort Park

far away from the rules of sea-faring    far far from
Gloucester

far by the rule of Ousoos    far where you carry

the color, Bulgar

far where Enyalion

quietly re-enters his Chariot    far

by the rule of its parts by the law of the proportion
of its parts

over the World    over the City    over man[10]

That seems to say what the image of the world, at least for me, has been.

I can, therefore, move, I believe, to what I there call history. And I'm happy to use the word to stand for city. [Writes on blackboard.] I mean, I'm nuts on numbers because it seems to me I'm a literalist. And I wished only to bracket these two, say, and these two hooked obviously by words alone. [Joins *imago mundi* to *anima mundi* and *orb* to *urb*.]

I mean the city of the earth, which as far as I know on this continent arose in Massachusetts, and was, as you all know, quoted by . . . in fact, the only time I found Mr. Kennedy interesting, verbally, was when he made his appearance, just after his successful election, before the General Court of Massachusetts. I don't know how many of you would have known that he, immediately after his victory, came to, appeared, and made a speech before the General Court of Massachusetts and quoted that remarkable phrase of Winthrop's: "that this colony shall shine like a city on a hill."[11] I may garble it, but some of you that know the speech may remember it. That's the one time I was moved by Mr. Kennedy. And a day after this previous poem I wrote this one. And I would like to use it to . . . I mean I'm excited by this series of four poems. They represent for me an outbreak of much that the *Maximus* had been approaching for me for the ten, fifteen previous years.

7 years & you cld carry cinders in yr hand
for what the country was worth broken
on the body
on the wheel of a new
body
a new social body

he was broken
on the wheel    his measure

was broken        Winthrop's

vision was broken he was broken the country

had walked away
                                        and the language
has belonged to trade or the English
ever since    until now once more J W

can be said to be able

to be listened to:  wanax

the High governor

of Massachusetts    John

wanax who imagined

that men

cared

for what kind of the world

they chose to

live in

and came here seeking

the possibility:  Good News

can come

from Canaan[12]

[Olson laughs.] OK. But I'm having so much fun [laughter] I would like to read "Some Good News," a poem in fivers that is this poem previously:

how small the news was
a permanent change had come
by 14 men setting down
on Cape Ann, on the westerly side
of the harbor

the same side Bradford,
the fall before, had asked London
to get for him
so that New Plymouth
could prosecute fishing, no place,

in the minds of men, England
or on the ground, equal,
and fitting the future
as this Cape sitting
between the old

North Atlantic (of Biskay,
and Breton, of Cabot's
nosing into, for Bristol)
and the new—Georges
(as the bank was called as early

as 1530: who gave her their
patron saint—England?
Aragon? or Portyngales?)
Or Old Man's Pasture, Tillies
Bank, whichever way

you take what advantage
Cape Ann: Levett
says "too faire a gloss"
is placed on her,
the same year

New Plymouth here,
Dorchester there,
and Levett himself,

at Quack, care
to be right. 1623,

all of them,
suddenly,
pay attention,
to what fishermen
(since when? before
1500) have

been showing: the motion
(the Westward motion)
comes here,
to land. Stations
(going back to sheep,
and goats on Sable

Island, of all sand spits
upon the globe, and terror
of blown or dragged or dropped
earth in the midst of
water—shoals, worse

than rock because
they do blow shift lie,
are changing as you sound—
on this crooked sand
Portuguese (when?)

had a fishing station.
It wasn't new,
what happened,
at Cape Ann. It's where,
and when it

did. Smith,
at Monhegan,
1614, and telling
about it, in a book.
1616, is

the demarcation (he,
the Sea-Marke!
as competently Columbus
backwards as Grant
forward, John Smith

the stater of
quantity and
precision, the double
doesn't unravel
so you'd know it

just like that, dragging,
as we do
shifty new
land, sucks
down, into the terrible

inert of
nature (the Divine
Inert, the literary man
of these men
of the West,

who knew private
passivity as these
quartermasters knew
supplies, said
it has to be

if princes
of the husting
are to issue from
the collapse
of the previous

soul: Smith,
too early yet
to be understood

to be the sign
of present

paternities—braggart
fisherman, the
Androgyne who hates
the simulacrum
Time Magazine

takes for male,
the playing coy
with identity)
a man's
struggle

with Caesar's
dream,
that he'd been intimate
with his mother,
and the soothsayer

eased him: it only means
that you shall conquer
the world. Smith,
as Sam Grant after,
was futile

until the place
and time burned
with the same heat as
the man (it isn't
for us to say

what a proper fire
is, it's what,
like Corinth
burning down
produces bronze—

or my Cabbage, we
baked potatoes
Fisher's Hill—or Caesar
dreamed, in Spain—or Smith,
who came to Monhegan

to catch whales,
found cod, instead.
And furs. And Frenchmen
ahead of him, west
of him. Yet

Smith
changed
everything: he pointed
out
Cape Ann,

named her
so it's stuck,
and Englishmen,
who were the ones
who wanted to,

sat down, planted
fisheries
so they've stayed put,
on this coast, from Pemaquid
to Cape Cod.

One needs
grab hold of,
with purchase
this purpose, that
the Continental Shelf

was Europe's
first West, it wasn't
Spain's

south:  fish,
and furs

and timber,
were wealth,
neither plants
old agricultural
growing, from

Neolithic, sickles
& that kind of
contemplation
of nature, she
the brooder

nor gold, and murder.
We kill
as a fisherman's
knife nicks
abundance.

Which we take
for granted,
we don't even earn
our labor (as patriarchy
and matriarchy)

we do it all
by quantity and
machine. The subjective
hides, or runs riot
("vainglorious,"

they put Smith down
as, and hire a Standish
to do corporative
murder:  keep things clean,
by campaigns

drop brombs. One cries Mongols
instead. Yet Grant

still is a name
for butcher, for how
he did finally hammer out
a victory over

Clotho Lee, the spinner
the stocking frame
undid:  textile
us, South
and North—the world,

tomorrow, and all
without fate
tomorrow,
if we,
who come from a housekeeping

which old mother Smith
started,
don't find out the inert
is as gleaming as,
and as fat as,

fish—so
we move:  sd the
literary man, from hidden places
sprang
the killer's
instrument

who is also
the boatsteerer.
The "lily-iron,"
they called the swordfish
harpoon when Gloucester

still chased
the blue-backed
thing on Browns (east
of Monhegan, north
of Georges

West
and south Smith
put down the claim;
and wrote
her paper
and her name

"The which
is riches
will change
the world" not knowing,
as we don't,

he'd hang up,
and be
a mark for all
who on this coast
do fall,

aloof aloof,
and come no near,
we cry. Or we'll over,
and you better
follow us who

from the hustings ("trash,"
industrial fish
are called which Gloucester
now catches, all that the bottom
of Georges,

the Channel, Middle Ground,
Browns, Pollock Rip

yields, anything
nature puts in the sea
comes up,

it is cornucopia
to see it
working up a sluggish
treadle,
from a ship's hold

to the truck
which takes it to the De-Hy
to be turned into catfood,
and fertilizer, for nature's
fields

Out of these waters
inland, it went. From then
—from Smith—some good news
better
get after[13]

[Applause.]

I'd rather like to read you one pair poem to that, and one that's the third of the set. To come back to the one I read you, I guess, like, as of what I consider both the city and ourselves. I don't know whether I can do this one too good. Why don't I jump the Winthrop poem[14] and go to the one that nobody, I think, seems to have been particularly interested in, but I'm so fond of it. These are all written in . . . I may have punched that out a little bit . . . but they're all written in what I call fivers, the three of them. And the third one is called "Capt. Christopher Levett (of York)." Quack, that reference in the previous poem, is the old name for Casco, the old pronunciation for Casco, and Casco is now Portland, and Christopher Levett was the first person to put down there.

Levett is a measure
—the writ, that 14 men
had sat down
at Cape Anne, did not run
to him, where Portland

was to be; and didn't get
to London, from the West
country. Levett says only,
1624, I left
some men myself, and Plymouth

people . . . Though that
Cape Ann led on
to Commonwealth, and Maine
stayed Maine,
is not the news. The news

which Levett had to tell
(as Conant might have)
was a simpler thing, of such import
an island's named today
"House Island"—and Conant's

house was timbers
in a city's stable
so few years back
I touched them, when a kid,
and didn't know it, the first ones

on an continent which men
have let go so our
eyes which look
to strike
take nothing

of even furthest previous
thought, local
national or new spatial

as tolerable. A man
who speaks as Levett does
of what he's done
("I have obtained a place
of habitation in New-

England, where I have built
a house, and fortified it
in a reasonable good fashion,
strong enough against such enemies
as are those Savage people")

speaks (as he does of each
new thing he saw and did
in these new parts) so we,
who live at this poor end
of goods, & thing, & men,

when materials, of each,
are such a man can't eat
sleep walk move go
apart from his own dwelling,
the dirtiness of goodness

cheapness shit is
upon the world. We'll turn
to keep our house, turn to
houses where our kind,
and hungry after them,

not willing to bear one short walk
more out into even what they've done
to earth itself, find
company. Since these two men
put down two houses

by fish flakes and stages
on rocks near water with trees
against sea—one's forced,
considering America,
to a single truth: the newness

the first men knew was almost
from the start dirtied
by second comers. About seven years

and you can carry cinders
in your hand for what

America was worth. May she be damned
for what she did so soon
to what was such a newing
that we, who out the side
of her come (have cut ourselves

out of her drugstore flattened-hillside gut
like Wash-Ching-Geka cut
the Winnebago nation out
of elephant—"the fish,
sd Levett, which we there saw,

some with wings, others with manes,
ears, heads, who chased
one another with open mouths
like stone Horses in a parcke"—
We have the gain. We know

what Levett Smith or Conant
didn't, that no one
knew better
than to cash in on it. Out,
is the cry of a coat of wonder[15]

That makes me feel as though I ought to jump right into neo-capitalism. I didn't realize I was putting *down* so much. I feel, as a matter of fact, that this later poem that I read you first, which let me now read like I'm summarizing. [Reads again "7 years & you cld carry cinders in yr hand." Applause.]

And now, if I believe that these two things are mundane and *these* two are the realer things, I'd like finally to end with the spirit of the world, which I have never been able to see as other than the figure of woman as she is such in the very phrase *anima mundi.* I will just read this fourth poem, fifth actually of the days that these poems were written, which is the translation I promised of this section from "The Song of Ullikummi."

For those of you who heard the poems I read in Vancouver, some of which have appeared in print since, the poem has also a connection previously. It would be impossible, I think, to read the actual transliteration. I'm actually translating the very first tablet of "The Song of Ullikummi."[16] It opens up on Kumarbi, father of all the gods:

> Of Kumarbi, father of all the gods, I shall sing.
>
> Kumarbi wisdom unto his mind takes,
> and a bad 'day,' as evil (being) he raises.
> And against the Storm-God evil he plans,
>
> And against the Storm-God a *rebel* he raises.
>
> Kumarbi wisdom unto his mind [takes],
> And like a bead he sticks it on.
>
> When Kumarbi wisdom unto his mind had taken,
> from (his) chair he promptly rose.
> Into (his) hand a staff he took,
> Upon his feet as shoes the swift winds he put.
>
> And from (his) town Urkis he set out,
> and to *ikunta luli* he came.
> And in *ikunta luli* a great rock lies:

And that's where I picked it up.

   fucked the Mountain
   fucked her but good    his mind
   sprang forward
and with the rock he slept
and into her he let his manhood
   go    five times    he let it go
            ten times    he let it go

      in ikunta luli    she is three
   dalugasti long
                  she is one and a half

palhasti wide. What below she has
up on this his mind sprang upon.

When Kumarbi his wisdom
he took upon
his mind
he took his istanzani
to his piran hattatar
istanzani piran daskizzi

Kumarbis -za istanzani piran hattatar
daskizzi
sticks wisdom
unto his mind like his cock
into her
iskariskizzi

the fucking
of the Mountain
fucked the Mountain
went right through it
and came out the other side

the father of all the gods
from his town Urkis
he set out
and to ikunta luli
he came

and in ikunta luli a great rock
lies
sallis perunas
kittari he came upon
What below she has
he sprang upon
with his mind
he slept
with the rock kattan sesta

with the peruni

and into her    misikan X-natur
andan    his manhood
flowed
into her

And five times he took her
nanzankan    5-anki das
and again ten times he took her
namma man zankan    10-anki das

Arunas
the Sea[17]

Thank you. [Applause.] I see I'm short. If anybody wants any more—not any more of that!—but I mean if this lecture isn't complete I can complete it.

RICHARD BAKER:

The clock is fifteen minutes slow.

CHARLES OLSON:

Oh, it is? Oh, good. [Laughter.]

RICHARD DUERDEN:

Could you give a different shot at that *anima mundi* as woman, did you say?

CHARLES OLSON:

Yeah, I just meant the rather classic figure, which I . . . well, for example in the Tarot deck it's the *El Mundo,* card XXI is *anima mundi.* She's the Virgin . . . she's the whole works. She's it.

QUESTION:

Well, why do you go to another culture to get your myth?

CHARLES OLSON:

Well, you knock me out if you say that. I just thought I bridged the cultures. [He laughs.] I don't believe in cultures myself. I think that's a lot of hung up stuff like organized anything. I believe there is simply ourselves, and where we are has a particularity which we'd better use because that's about all we got. Otherwise we're running around looking for somebody else's stuff. But that particularity is as great as numbers are in arithmetic. The literal is the same as the numeral to me. I mean the literal is an invention of language and power the same as numbers. And so there is no other culture. There is simply the literal essence and exactitude of your own. I mean, the streets you live on, or the clothes you wear, or the color of your hair is no different from the ability of, say, Giovanni di Paolo to cut the legs off Santa Clara or something. Truth lies solely in what you do with it. And that means *you.* I don't think there's any such thing as a creature of a culture.

I think we live so totally in an acculturated time that the reason why we're all here that care and write is to put an end to that whole thing. Put an end to nation, put an end to culture, put an end to divisions of all sorts. And to do this you have to put establishment out of business. It's just a structure of establishment. And my own reason for being, like I said, on the left side and being so hung up on form is that I feel that today, as much as action, the invention . . . not the invention, but the *discovery* of formal structural means is as legitimate as, *is* for me the form of action. The radical of action lies in finding out how organized things are genuine, are initial, to come back to that statement I hope I succeeded in making about the *Imago mundi.* That *that's* initial in any of us. We have our picture of the world and *that's* the creation.

I mean with some deliberateness I should expose myself. I shrank everything that I feel and know about mythology into those four in order to offer today, to you, at least, that best shrinkage I know at this moment. Is that fair?

ROBERT DUNCAN:

Charles, I think I can swing back to—that as poets we have to find the term that stands for what we have known that's there. And it might go all the way back to, I mean I certainly, this last one goes back to the one place you found where it is. You know.

CHARLES OLSON:

Yeah. That's right.

ROBERT DUNCAN:

Now you don't care if you found it yesterday. You found it there. So you have to go there.

CHARLES OLSON:

That's right.

ROBERT DUNCAN:

And you recognize that, you read through miles and you recognize that this thing's it.

CHARLES OLSON:

Yeah. That's all. And believe you me I know everyone has their own recognitions, which Duncan knows so well too. This is one of the exciting things about something that the word "myth" used to mean. And it's a big drag to use it. But like I say I found, in fact—I've got a poem in this new book: "wrote my first essay on myth, like at Kent Kunt circle." It's that dipolar for me. I find that what we call mythology is the inclusion of all this that you're speaking of. The *recognition*. And I don't believe there is a single person in this room that doesn't have the opportunity—the absolute place and thing that's theirs. I mean places and things that are theirs. That's again why I say I think the literal is the same as the numeral. I don't believe that everyone of us isn't absolutely *specific*. And *has* his specificity.

I don't know what your use of the word "analysis" is and the words you use, but I would use the other word reductive. The *reductive* is what I'm proposing. I don't think you can get your recognitions by going out. I think they come by going—from within. That sounds too easy to say it . . .

I do want to, really, use that papal blessing which I still, as a Catholic, am impressed by. You do all know that, that after his election each pope is required to come to that door, in that horrible building by Michelangelo and Raphael, and bless the city and the world. And I really . . . I mean, that moves me, like. That's why I'd say the mundane is recognizable too. [Writes on blackboard.] And the other bracket, which I do put on the left don't I, is that one.

And I don't mind proving . . . I mean it's fun to do this today, to take poems and do what nobody—I mean, just let them be proof. Test them as proof. I think poems and actions both should stand that. If they fall down then it's our intellectualism only that's been exposed.

QUESTION:

Which of these mythological elements do you think the establishment, trade, and war is an expression of?

CHARLES OLSON:

I would say that when it comes to war, you have beauty. That's why I read . . . let me put those poems [writing on board], or let me put him where he belongs, as Enyalion. And trade would be certainly this . . . and politics would certainly be Mr. John Wanax of Massachusetts. By the way, if anyone thinks I'm being obscure there, or writing like an advertisement for Johnson, wanax is the linear B name for high king of Mycenae. Agamemnon was wanax of the forces at Troy.

What do you do with this woman poem, this screw poem? *Ikunta luli.* Yeah. I got you though. I answered you. Really. Trade? Yeah. The earth is . . . *goods!* That beautiful thing. We have and we now have produced—I mean man, the world can have, everybody can have goods today.

This thing is . . . I would take, I mean just take that great Blake statement. This is his "ugly," this is his "reason." This is his Urizen. Isn't it? Sure it is. Al, isn't that Urizen? Sure. Trade. The earth is Urizen. I mean he was as clear-headed on reason and the rational as anybody I know. Well, I answered you, I think, huh?

COMMENT:

Yes, I think so.

CHARLES OLSON:

And I would say, by the way I would, oh, that was what I wanted to do on the Blake thing. This is the fourth, I think that Blake doesn't mention, and says the four constitute the son of God. I swear he does. You know he's got a marvelous blank there. He just doesn't finish his fourth part of man. The ugly, the beautiful, the strong, and the . . . constitute the four who is the son of God. And he doesn't mean that the fourth is the son of God. He obviously doesn't.

Well, the clock is fifteen minutes slow, so it's after twelve. Thanks. [Applause.]

NOTES:

[1]"Two Sections from *Maximus," Paris Review,* VIII, 32 (Summer-Fall 1964), pp. 76–77.

[2]Frances Rose-Troup: *The Massachusetts Bay Company and Its Predecessors* (New York, 1930).

[3]*The Maximus Poems* (New York, 1960), pp. 147–48.

[4]*Ibid.*, pp. 148–51.

[5]*Ibid.*, p. 151.

[6]*Ibid.*, p. 146.

[7]"Two Sections from *Maximus," op. cit.*

[8]Henry Corbin: *Avicenna and the Visionary Recital* (New York, 1960), p. 148.

[9]William Blake: *The Complete Writings*, edited by Geoffrey Keynes (London, 1957), pp. 577–81: "A Descriptive Catalogue of Pictures . . . 1809, Number V":

*The Ancient Britons*

*In the last Battle of King Arthur, only Three Britons escaped; these were the Strongest Man, the Beautifullest Man, and the Ugliest Man; these three marched through the field unsubdued, as Gods, and the Sun of Britain set, but shall arise again with tenfold splendor when Arthur shall awake from sleep, and resume his dominion over earth and ocean.*

> The three general classes of men who are represented by the most Beautiful, the most Strong, and the most Ugly, could not be represented by any historical facts but those of our own country, the Ancient Britons, without violating costume. The Britons (say historians) were naked civilized men, learned, studious, abstruse in thought and contemplation; naked, simple, plain in their acts and manners; wiser than after-ages. They were overwhelmed by brutal arms, all but a small

remnant; Strength, Beauty, and Ugliness escaped the wreck,
and remain for ever unsubdued, age after age. . . .

The Strong Man represents the human sublime. The Beautiful Man represents the human pathetic, which was in the wars of Eden divided into male and female. The Ugly Man represents the human reason. They were originally one man, who was fourfold; he was self-divided, and his real humanity slain on the stems of generation, and the form of the fourth was like the Son of God. How he became divided is a subject of great sublimity and pathos. The Artist has written it under inspiration, and will, if God please, publish it; it is voluminous, and contains the ancient history of Britain and the world of Satan and of Adam. . . .

The strong Man acts from conscious superiority, and marches on in fearless dependance on the divine decrees, raging with the inspirations of a prophetic mind. The Beautiful Man acts from duty and anxious solicitude for the fates of those for whom he combats. The Ugly Man acts from love of carnage, and delight in the savage barbarities of war, rushing with sportive precipitation into the very jaws of the affrighted enemy. . . .

[10]*Coyote's Journal,* No. 8 (1967), pp. 1–4.

[11]John Winthrop, "Modell of Christian Charity." Recently quoted in Page Smith: *As a City Upon a Hill* (New York, 1966), p. 6: "For we must consider that we shall be as a city upon a hill. The eyes of all people are upon us . . ."

[12]"Two Sections from *Maximus*," *op. cit.*

[13]*The Maximus Poems,* pp. 120–27.

[14]"Stiffening, in the Master Founders' Wills," *Ibid.,* pp. 128–32.

[15]*Ibid.,* pp. 133–35.

[16]"The Song of Ullikummi," translated by Hans Güterbock, *Journal of Cuneiform Studies,* Vol. V, No. 4 (1951), pp. 135–61, and Vol. VI, No. 1 (1952), pp. 8–42.

[17]*City Lights Journal,* No. 3 (1966), pp. 147–48.